About the Author

I am a mental health nurse working within the NHS. I am a mother and grandmother and have never considered myself to achieve the status of published author, however this sudden news of the death of our George inspired me as if I was almost compelled to write for him and his fans. I consider myself to be a very down to earth family woman who loves to care for others hence my career path into nursing, yet here I am publishing a poetry book. I also work in the aesthetics industry on a part time basis and although I love my career, I just wished that I could have helped George with his demons. Obviously, I never got that opportunity but I help and have successfully helped others recover from severe mental disorders

I've loved my career in nursing and I like to think that the care that I have given, and continue to deliver, is valued as much as George's legacy.

We Too Have Died

Victoria Rowe

We Too Have Died

Olympia Publishers
London

www.olympiapublishers.com
OLYMPIA PAPERBACK EDITION

A CIP catalogue record for this title is
available from the British Library.

ISBN: 978-1-78830-016-2

First Published in 2018

Olympia Publishers
60 Cannon Street
London
EC4N 6NP

Printed in Great Britain

Dedication

I would like to dedicate this book to George's loyal fans from all over the world. You have experienced my pain and heartache at the loss of such an amazing, humble human being. To his family and friends and all who knew him personally, I hope that you take great comfort from knowing that you are not alone in your loss, the title says it all, '*We too have died*'.

Acknowledgments

Thank you to my beautiful daughters and grandchildren who have made me smile through my sadness. Also to the loss of my parents, my brother and sister-in-law, Paul and Bev, who have helped me to write this poetry, through losing you both too, it has been a roller coaster of emotions. To my sister Sue and brother-in-law, Don, thank you from the bottom of my heart. I would like to mention my work colleagues too, who laughed and thought that I was delusional throughout, yet this inspired me more. Also to my friend, Linda, who without her help in many ways this would never have been possible. I love you all so much.

When George Michael passed away the whole world was in shock, it was very hard to accept that our amazing entertainer would no longer be here with us, entertaining us, writing his compassionate music that he always wrote from the depth of his heart.

The first few days were surreal; it was almost as if we were in denial. We could not accept that George would no longer be around.

Social media sites were set up in his memory one of which I became a member of, this site was called GM Lovelies.

All the fans poured out their grief over the loss of their idol, the admiration and respect this man had from the whole world was hard to believe.

He was known to millions of people around the world for his contributions to the music industry. It was from becoming a member of this site that I became almost compelled to write poetry, the poetry came not just from my heart, but I realised the emotions that I was experiencing were the same as everyone else's around the world.

I began adding poetry on the site and his fans were making comments, almost as if they had written the same words. They were so thankful of the way in which I could express the feelings of his fans from every corner of the world.

I was then asked if I would consider writing a book

in George's memory as a tribute from us all.

It was quite scary that I was awakening in the early hours of the morning with poems in my head; I began to write as if our George guided me, his style of writing suddenly became my style.

Within forty days, I had written as many poems.

This book is the end result of my, our, forty days of hurt and pain.

I do hope that you will enjoy the experience and maybe you can relate and attach your emotions to the majority of the poems.

I am donating a percentage of all sales to George's charities in his memory.

I hope you all get as much pleasure from reading these as I did writing them.

I do not intend any of the speculation within some of the poems to offend anyone, these were written before we were notified of the outcome of his death,

We Too Have Died

Can it ever be possible to feel like; we too have died?
To feel the hole inside our hearts, to dry the tears we
have cried.
We honestly can say these are feelings deep within,
We would like to tell you all about them, but where do
we begin?
Maybe from that Christmas night, when we heard the
tragic news.
How could this be possible? That was we, your
lovelies', views
You know what, ever since that night,
Our life on Earth just doesn't seem right.
The pain is greater every day,
We want you back with us to stay.
You touched our lives, George, that is one thing for
sure,
We know that as the hurt inside every day, hurts some
more.
We listen to your voice and we're so thankful that we
can,
Because we cherish the music left from you and from
Wham.

We wonder if you're happy up there in heaven above,
We wonder if you're aware of just how much you're
loved.
Can you see our eyes? They no longer glisten,
They are full of pain and sorrow, as each of us lovelies
listen.
To the heartbreak we all are sharing, and the pain we
can no longer bare,
When we think that you are not with us in life, but in the
sky somewhere.
If someone had told us that the pain would be this great,
We truly wouldn't have believed them; we are all in
such a state.
We're never going to dance again,
You are the only one to stop our tears.
To lose you, it cuts like a knife,
We now know the meaning of these words you wrote in
life.
God bless you George, may you finally rest in peace,
Whilst we, your lovelies, will hopefully ease.
The pain in our hearts, the pain in our mind,
As we cherish the memories of one of a kind.

On My Mind

It is four in the morning,
We are so tired and we can't stop yawning.
Yet again we are wide-awake and asking ourselves why,
We wake up so early and all we do is cry.
Then the harsh reality suddenly comes to our head,
That you're not coming back George, because you're up
in heaven instead.
We toss and turn, we start to cry,
We keep on asking why, why, why.
Surely, dear lord, you didn't need him as much as we
did here,
If only you could give him back, if just for another year.
But then we think of all the hurt that we are going
through,
Could we really grieve again over the loss of you?
Sometimes we think we are selfish, wanting you back
with us here,
But George we just can't take much more, we do wish
our minds were clear.
The song that's playing in our head, is the one that we
can't bear to hear,
It's *Last Christmas,* this will never be the same, its one

song that we fear.
It will provoke so many memories,
Of that fateful cruel night.
When you went to bed all alone, with no one by your
side.
Why do we feel so empty? We are no longer whole,
And all because that cold winters night, something or
someone stole,
Our beloved legend our beautiful treasure,
Who whilst here on earth gave so much pleasure.
Please forgive us as we weep,
We really wish that we could sleep.
As tomorrow is yet another day,
To feel the pain since you went away

A Message from Our George

I'm standing at the gates of heaven, but I just can't seem
to go in,
And that's because I'm looking down and all you
lovelies appear so grim.
Please don't mourn my passing and don't judge me for
my death,
I think I suffered enough, my last few years on earth.
I am sad that you all cry for me, that just wasn't my
intent,
Please try and be happy for the time that I had spent.
My music it all came from the experiences in my life,
I wrote it from my heart and wanted it to be kind.
I never got to experience the paternal love of a child,
Maybe that's what I should have done instead of running
wild.
But my lovelies please don't be so sad,
Because the life I had, really wasn't that bad.
I know that there's one thing that I believe I did do
right,
That was to leave you all my music to listen day and
night.
So you now have my memories to cherish in your

hearts,
And my music that you can listen to, every Sunday in
the charts.
As I'm sure that you will now buy more,
When my new material is released in store.
I'm sorry that it hurts so much,
Please forgive me and feel my last touch.
Before I enter into the pearly gates,
To be reunited with some of my mates.
I know my mum is waiting there and she quite possibly
could be cross,
So I'll have to speak with all the other legends that you
lost.
I want you all to celebrate with my music sing and
dance,
Because as you know now I will no longer get that
chance.
When my funeral takes place just remember that it is my
shell,
Because I'm already up in heaven, I may have been bad
but, I somehow managed to escape hell.
So, from that take your comfort,
And remember what I said.
Because while ever you all live,
I'll never really be dead.
Now I've told you that, it is time for me to rest,
Thank you all, my lovelies, you really are the best.

The Brits

Andrew, Pepsi and Shirley we his lovelies want to say,
Thank you from our broken hearts, for what you did
today.
You delivered your eulogy straight from your hearts,
This must have been so painful and difficult to start.
But you continued to deliver, in spite of all your pain,
You had to stop a few times as the tears they fell like
rain.
As we watched you on the stage it was difficult to see,
As there used to be the four of you and there were now
only three.
We can only imagine how hurt you really are,
As George was like your family and now he's gone so
far.
In our minds we picture him stood right by you on the
stage,
If only this was true, but we've now turned a different
page.
If only he could see just how much hurt he's left behind,
He then would maybe realise, that he was one of a kind.
You three should be thankful for the time that you all
spent,

As you had him with you many years, we only had him
lent.
His music and his charm, his cheeky little grin,
Will be the wonderful memories that we all cherish of
him.
But once again we thank-you for what you did that
night,
The tribute was amazing you all got it just right.
We would like to thank the producer, who set it up so
well,
He too must have loved George, that was clear to tell.
Then we too must thank Chris he did his very best,
It couldn't have been easy to compete with all the rest.
When George began to sing, it broke our hearts in two,
As we expected him walking on stage, but that was
impossible to do.
The tribute left, we his fans, realising that he's gone,
How the hell are we expected to just keep moving on?
Please, please dear gods up above, please help us heal
our pain,
As the way we are feeling right now, we will never love
again.
George was irreplaceable of that there is no doubt,
But we his fans are in so much pain, the grief has wiped
us out.
No more pleasure, no more smiles, no more future, no
more joy,
Our lives have been so miserable since God stole our
perfect boy.

Your Girls

It takes a special person to genuinely love a dog,
But we your fans could see that this was you Yog.
Wherever you went and whatever dog you saw,
You always went to stroke it and hold its little paw.
You were so very special a wonderful beautiful guy,
We just cannot imagine you ever telling a lie.
You know that dogs are loyal to the one that shows
them love,
So, god knows how she's coping, now you're in heaven
above.
Because we who weren't a part of your life aren't coping
very well,
So, we just can't imagine the stories your family will
tell,
Of a loyal, caring, kind, considerate, humanitarian
talented man,
Whose fame and fortune started with the duo *Wham*.
The whole world is in mourning that you are no longer
here,
Your presence here on earth will be sorely missed each
year.
We can only imagine you in heaven above,

Surrounded by the ones you love.
But we just wish you were still around,
With us here on earth safe and sound.
We miss you George Michael, and always will,
So please rest your worn out weary soul until,
We meet again up above,
And smother you with all our love.

The Pain in Our Hearts

The pain in our hearts becomes more unbearable every
day,
Can anyone find the answer as to why you couldn't
stay?
We've never been so traumatised by the loss of a
superstar,
Your passing has been the hardest, most definitely by
far.
We have no more strength to carry on here alone,
Without our beloved, George, who now calls heaven
home.
Tears fall from our eyes and roll right down our cheeks,
As time goes by, it doesn't get any easier, it's the same
pain every week.
We've never been so shocked as the day that you left us
all,
That Christmas Day is one day, we won't ever want to
recall.
Your songs will play within our hearts and remain deep
in our minds,
As You were definitely unique just one of a kind.
We wish we could have understood just what was in

your head,
We would have tried to help you; we feel you were
misled.
But no it isn't happy times, we write from deep inside,
It's heartbreak for our lovely George, with tears that
we've all cried.
If loving could have saved you George, you never
would have died.

Realisation

Well George, the Brits just reinforced what we didn't
want to accept,
Because as you know George, you're the one real guy
we wish we could have kept.
Andrew, Pepsi and Shirley paid tribute to you well,
They truly, truly loved you that were clear to tell.
There were tears flowing from all of your fans,
Wondering who was coming on to sing for our man.
Then it started, Chris did his best but it just wasn't you,
Then your voice came in and we asked, 'could it be
true?'
We thought that you were there and it all had been a
dream,
But reality hit us hard, our eyes started to stream.
It's over George, you're really not coming back,
The pain is so intense; our hearts are about to crack.
If only, if only this wasn't true,
There will never be another you.
Goodbye George wasn't what we ever wanted to say,
But we will meet again in heaven one day.
We love you George, we really, really do,
Your lovelies thought the world of you.
Forever and ever you will be in our hearts,
Until we too from this world depart.

From Heaven to My Dad

I'm watching you from heaven father and sending you
my love,
This wasn't how it was meant to be, me in heaven
above.
We may have had our differences throughout our lives
on earth,
But you know what, I am missing you I never
appreciated your worth.
Think about me father, as I'm sure you always do,
It's beautiful up here; mum sends her love too.
I wished things could have been different, it really
wasn't my time,
I had so much planned for the coming months; it was
my time to shine.
I loved you so much father, and I really wanted you to
know,
I wanted to thank you for everything, I wanted us to
grow.
But unfortunately, we couldn't be together any more,
God called me to his kingdom; on earth I closed the
door.
I imagine you're all hurting and missing me so much,

Just cherish all the happy times and feel my gentle
touch.
My mother is here right by my side, she's been waiting
far too long,
She's missed me so much so, I'm writing her a song.
She says it's time for us to go now, we've got so much to
do,
So until you come to see us, just to say we both love
you.

George   .

As we listen to your music and we hear your beautiful
voice,
Deep inside we began to feel the pain, but we know that
it's our choice.
Yet every day we cause ourselves so much heartache
and more pain,
As we listen to your meaningful words over and over
again.
In the corner of our eyes there is a glisten of a tear,
But we will continue to listen year after year.
It's really still so hard George, to accept that you have
left us,
And we know that deep in our hearts you wouldn't have
wanted a fuss.
Yet, somehow we feel there's a need deep inside us all,
That we want to pay you back for all the memories great
and small.
We really can't put into words just what our grief
entails,
For the loss of our one true love, our beautiful sexy
male.
Night after night, day after day, life is becoming a

struggle,

Work is becoming more difficult, we're sorry if we are much trouble.

But how will we ever come to terms with losing someone we loved?

Every time we see you we become so moved.

If you could write a song now for all your loyal fans,

We have a feeling that it would be of your future plans.

We're sure that you won't be angry if your new material was released,

Or the documentary that you nearly finished was to be screened on our TV.

We really can't put into words our pain our sadness and despair,

Since Christmas Day 2016 when we were told that you're no longer there.

You loved your home in Goring, you were so proud to show it off,

We remember when you were on Oprah, you showed her your favourite stuff.

You also showed us Nu your wonderful housemaid,

How lucky she must have felt when her boss had it played.

We never saw her role advertised in the press or even on the net,

Because George you would have been interviewing all your life, of that I can bet.

Imagine the privilege that all your staff have had,

To have had the incredible honour of working for you, now they are so sad.

We just want the house to stay right where it is, we don't want it to be sold,

Then hopefully when the pain begins to heal, it will be
used as something bold.
Maybe it could be made into something like Princes
Paisley Park,
And the revenue that it receives can be shared out to the
charities of your heart.
O dear lord please forgive us as tears fill our eyes each
day,
But we really are struggling since our idol went away.
Goodbye George, even that is hard to write,
So maybe we will just say something not as final and
that is goodnight.

Life Changes

Life has changed so very much because you are no
longer here,
When we get up in the morning, there seems to be no
cheer.
O god why are the days becoming so hard to bare?
Just knowing deep within our hearts that you're no
longer there.
If only the thoughts, the hurt, the pain, was easy to
express,
But it's not George, it's getting harder my god, it's such a
mess.
We absolutely can't explain the hurt we are going
through,
Because dear George, we have to say we really do love
you.
There is no more motivation, no pleasure here, just pain,
Our minds can't rest we're irritable and feel like we're
going insane.
We try watching you on TV, we try reading all your
books,
But George that's not what we want, it's you, your voice,
your looks.

We wonder if there will be a day when the pain will
eventually subside,
Because we your lovelies cry every single night.
We cannot forget you George and perhaps we never
will,
Until the day we die, you will be with us still.
If only you knew how much we cared,
If only our love could have been evenly shared.
We feel that these gestures albeit small,
May have helped you to still be here with us all.
We are heartbroken George there's a hole here on earth,
You were loved so much from the day of your birth.

For Nu

This is for George's housekeeper, Nu,
My god, I bet he thought the world of you.
You were so privileged to be with him there,
I bet he displayed just how much he cared.
You must be so upset for the loss of your dear friend,
Who would ever have thought that this would have been
the end.
I just wish you would have been there on that Christmas
Eve,
But then I guess you had family; therefore, had to leave.
It really must be hard having to potter around his home,
I wonder, do you feel his presence when you are alone?
You must be so envied by all of his loyal fans,
To having spent that precious time even if some of it
was scrubbing pans.
I can't imagine just at this moment what you're going
through,
But I can imagine Nu he thought the world of you.
You must have so many stories of what you would like
to tell,
But respecting his family, is your priority we know that
well.

I hear you have collected tributes from us all outside his
home,
And that you're planning to save them for his family,
you're such a caring soul.
I came down to Goring from Yorkshire on New Year's
Eve,
I cried so much I didn't want to leave.
I was interviewed by the local TV news,
I'm now on YouTube; had lots of views.
I just wish that day when I came down, that George
would have been home,
It was so surreal to think that you were in his home
alone.
His house is stunning, the village is so quaint,
I became overwhelmed and felt quite faint.
There were many people visiting to pay their respects,
I spoke to many people, who I had never met.
I wonder if George knew just how much he was loved,
I wish we could get the message to him up above.
But to you Nu from a broken hearted fan,
I want to thank you from the bottom of my heart for
taking care of our man.
Can you pass a message to the gardeners, who are
planning to place the plants,
In George's garden all around as tributes from his fans?
I really think that this idea has been so well thought,
His fans are so honoured that you've used the things we
bought.
Once again please accept my heartfelt sympathy,
For the loss of our wonderful George who meant the
world to me.

Your Lewd Act

It was a Wednesday in April 1988,
When the world was informed that day of your fete.
You were caught in a toilet with another guy,
We think you were set up, but that's by the by.
We weren't embarrassed and didn't love you any less,
You had disguised your sexuality, why was it portrayed
as such a mess?
We loved you George we really didn't mind,
That you preferred guys, was it difficult to find?
Were you really afraid of telling your mum?
She surely wouldn't have minded, as you were her only
son.
The press, they tried to do their best to portray you as a
fool,
But you pulled it off very well George, and acted rather
cool.
I'm not sure if you were fond of all your fortune and
your fame,
But then I guess we understand, as at times the press
weren't tame.
We really wish you would have asked your fans for
some advice,

We could have given you answers; you wouldn't have
had to think twice.
But that all past some years ago and you eventually
became free,
Of all the nasty journalists just waiting for a fee.
We don't mind George we never have, we are just glad
that you came out,
Because you got to love some wonderful men, of that
there is no doubt.

Melanie and Yioda

Melanie and Yioda, I just wanted you to know,
I feel your pain every day, it just won't go.
The reason I can empathise is really very clear,
It's because I too lost my brother just the other year.
He was only fifty-five, he had a heart attack, it was a
shock,
But he wasn't famous, although he was funny and boy
could he rock.
It's a very similar story that has happened to us all,
And a very sad ending to your brother George and my
brother Paul.
He went to bed that fateful night saying he was in a bit
of pain,
But he wouldn't have the doctor, and he never woke up
again.
I bet your going through all the emotions, anger, denial
and guilt,
Probably feeling emotionally detached, there's a lot of
gaps to fill.
I work in the NHS, I work in mental health,
I just wish that George could have been helped
exclusive of his wealth.

I've been down to mill cottage and was interviewed by
the local news,
Then I placed my eulogy on the door I hope you read it,
it's sure to amuse.
You must miss your brother dearly and the pain must be
so sore,
But it does get a little easier, even though now it is so
raw.
Please wipe your tears and look above,
And smile at George, your one true love,
He was your wonderful talented brother,
Who is now safe with your much-adored mother.
We his fans, do share your grief,
I know right now that's no relief.
But gentle George, who is up above,
Has had so much unconditional love.
I just wish that he would have known,
Then he wouldn't have died all-alone.
God bless you both try ease your pain,
Until you finally meet again.

Emotions

The day we heard the news that you had sadly passed,
We could not believe that this Christmas was to be your
last.
We your fans have found it really, really rough,
We have experienced every emotion that has been so
tough.
ANGER that you went away,
SADNESS that you are not here today.
HAPPINESS that you peacefully slept,
GUILTY that we never met.
We wish we could explain to you,
What we all are going through.
We never want to feel this again,
We've never experienced quite as much pain.
We feel so helpless. just what can we do,
Only pray that now you're as good as new.
That you're resting up in heaven above,
That your mother is showering you with all her love.
We as loyal fans will always ask the question why,
Our idol, our legend had to die.
If only we could have you back with us right here on
earth,

Then you would probably understand just how much
you were worth.

Goodnight our beautiful George
We love you so very much.

Accessing Therapies

I am a mental health nurse and often wonder if there
was anything that I could have done,
I've pondered over and over in my mind,
Believe me it hasn't been fun.
I utilize a therapy that I believe is one of the best,
It's called experiential therapy and it is unlike all the
rest.
The client and the therapist sit together side by side,
Then the both of them have to relax and close their eyes.
The therapist begins to ask what the clients are going
through,
Then as they speak, she in turn try's to experience what
they do.
It doesn't involve eye contact, which most people try to
avoid,
Because it's very personal but we try not to exploit.
I think you would have liked this George, I'm not sure if
you had tried,
But maybe if you had, then you possibly wouldn't have
died.
Therapies, non-medical treatments are what we do
prefer to use,

We add in antidepressants but there not there to abuse.
We advise not to drink alcohol, as this is a depressant,
So to stick with our interventions, may not have been so
pleasant.
But this is just not possible now, as you're not here to
try,
I Just wished we could have helped you, then you
wouldn't have had to die.

Drug Driving

Many people know that the 4th of July is American
Independence Day,
But we your fans remember it in a much more solemn
way.
It was on the news yet again about your drug addiction,
Why couldn't they just leave you be, instead of causing
so much friction?
You weren't the only person in the world to drive whilst
using drugs,
But you were made so public, why didn't this happen to
the thugs?
We knew that you were sorry for what you did that day,
And that you were so grateful that people were not in
your way.
But you were punished, you did your time,
We were so upset that you were sent down the line.
We wondered how you coped in there it couldn't have
been nice,
But you must have learned your lesson, you didn't go in
twice.
We your fans stood by you through all the good and
bad,

And that's because we really are the best fans you ever
had.
We loved and admired you George; you had our respect,
And that would never change no matter what, or who
you wrecked.
Come back to us please George all is forgiven,
We want you back on earth with us so we can continue
living.

My Brother

2012 was a very bad year for me,
I lost my wonderful brother he too had been set free.
He went to bed George, just like you,
And we his family didn't have a clue.
His girlfriend heard him make a noise,
She dashed out of bed to ring his boys.
When she turned on the light and looked in the bed,
She saw that my brother was already dead.
She called the paramedics and they worked on him so
hard,
His heart started to beat again but his brain was already
starved.
They took him to the hospital he was in intensive care,
But we got to say goodbye whilst they kept him there.
I have so many memories of my brother,
I loved him like no other.
He was fifty-five,
Just wish he were still alive.
We used to listen to your music back in the day,
Then we used to sing your songs and then we used to
play.
He was George and I was Shirley,

We didn't look like you two, he was skinny and my hair
was curly.
But we played your music all the time,
We knew the words line by line.
I get great comfort now; I know it's really grim,
But I know you're up in heaven singing songs to him.
He lost his wife eight years before,
And she loved you even more.
So, now that you have joined them up above,
Sing and dance I'm sure they will love,
To see you in concert up in the sky,
Because we're all awaiting that when we die.
So, until it's our turn we continue to see,
Your concerts on our DVD.
We loved you George and always will,
Our hearts still break and our eyes still fill.
With tears that fall upon our cheeks,
Why or why do we still feel so weak.
Forgive us please that we continue to cry,
But we really want one answer and that is WHY?
You left us all on that tragic night,
You picked up your wings and took the flight,
To the pearly gates in heaven above,
Good night, God bless George from your fans with love.

Broken Hearted

We can shout from the rooftops, we can scream from
our lungs,
But it breaks our heart to know that you'll never come.
We your fans are in so much pain,
It feels like we're living in a world full of rain.
That the sun will never shine so bright,
That our days will seem like it's always the night.
That wherever we go, whatever we do,
We will always have reminders of you.
If we as your fans are in so much distress,
Then your family and friends must be such a mess.
How can we ever recover?
From losing our idol, our legend our brother.
When we hear your music or see your beautiful face,
It triggers our memory that you will never be replaced.
So, how do we continue with the rest of our days,
I just can't see; we feel like we're in a maze.
As we think of you, as we often do,
We still wish that it just were not true.
Because our lives all changed so much, the day that we
lost you,
And if we could fetch you back, that is just what we
would do.

Our Pain

Sometimes we your fans just need to cry,
To express our emotions around why did you die.
What can we do what can we say?
Is there more pain waiting for another day?
We thought that with every passing day,
The pain would ease and just not stay.
But how wrong can our expectations be,
For the loss of a man that has wondered free.
Free from the media, free from the press,
That only took interest when things were a mess.
They never wanted news of the good in your life,
Especially when you didn't want to choose a wife.
What was so wrong, George, what could it be?
Did they not know about diversity?
Why couldn't they leave you to live with your choice?
To just be happy listening to your beautiful voice.
But no, they couldn't leave you they made money from
your fame,
From writing about your breakups to taking crack
cocaine.
We wonder if you could return, that they would do the
same,

Because all the tabloids wanted was someone to blame.
The reality has hit us now because all of your fans,
Are no longer watching you in concert instead we're making plans.
To travel to London to say our goodbyes,
To our beautiful George who we never thought would die.
We are hoping that you are somewhere above,
That your mind is at rest and there is plenty of love.
You can forget your addictions, be glad that they've gone,
And for us here on earth, your memory will live on.
At least we have found comfort in the love of each other,
And you have found yours back in the arms of your dear mother.
So find a big soft pillow George to rest your head upon,
As for us each day gets harder as we can't accept you're gone.

Broken Hearted

Gorgeous Georgios in heaven above,
Please accept all our love.
Don't be sad that we on earth grieve,
But we really didn't want you to leave.
We loved you, you see, so very much,
You were part of our teenage crush.
Each day we see your beautiful face,
Then we wonder why you had to race.
Up to heaven way too soon,
To be the brightest star next to the moon.
This world will never be the same,
Because every time we hear your name.
It's almost as if there's a knife in our hearts,
Twisting and stabbing then it all starts.
The memories of that Christmas Day,
When we all heard you had been taken away.
It was the news, we your fans, never wanted to hear,
Because we always wanted you very near.
So George please look down from heaven above,
Look at our grief in our outpouring of love.
Because now we know we will never be the same,
Whenever we hear your beautiful name.

Georgios kyriacos Panayiotou,
We will always be in love with you, 1963-2016

My Arrival

Well my fans I wanted to tell,
I did arrive in heaven and not in hell.
As I entered into the beautiful place,
My mother was there with a smile on her face.
I thought that she would be so mad,
But she was happy and I was glad.
She walked me around heaven; it's beautiful here,
I was so surprised when I heard a cheer.
I looked around and what did I see,
David Bowie smiling at me.
At the side of him was our legend Amy,
Then Michael and prince, Freddie and Whitney.
We're composing wonderful music, with meaningful
lyrics as well,
But were unsure how we can produce it, if you find out
then please tell.
You see you have all been emotionally distraught,
But we're all here together, so it's just a thought.
That you can all rest now that you know I'm really not
afraid,
My only regret is that I couldn't have stayed.
Goodbye my lovelies please remember me,
But like I said, don't be upset, it's my time to wander
free.

Our Worry

Do we think it's going to get easier and we will be free
from pain?
Or do the rest of you feel as though we are really going
insane?
Crushed, broken, hurt and raw,
Can we fans really take much more?
My god the suspense is hard to bare,
Is anyone bothered, does anyone care?
Where is our George, where has he gone?
Why has the funeral taken so long?
Am I the one who seems to think, the family didn't want
a fuss?
And he's been buried privately partly to protect us.
I really hope this is not the case,
I'm looking every day and trying to chase.
The news as its given to the world,
But not a whisper, not a word.
Sometimes my tears fall every day,
Can my pain not go away?
You as fans must empathies,
We are all full of knowledge and very wise.
My anxiety is increasing,

My heart is quickly beating.
Please whoever is holding the news, don't leave it very
much longer,
Because we fans can't take much more, we are not
getting any stronger.
Let us know right away,
When it is his burial day.
Because until he is placed next to his mum,
We are in suspense of what is to come.
Please consider his loyal fans as,
We're waiting to make important plans.

Goring Town

It was a very sad day in Goring town,
I didn't know what to expect as I travelled down.
My stomach; it was all in knots, I was anxious and
afraid,
As I pulled up and parked the car, I looked over for your
maid.
There were tributes strewn across the lawn,
I could not believe; my heart was torn.
George, my tears they started to flow, they came at such
a pace,
They continued to fall so freely, all the way down my
face.
I looked around me it was so surreal,
There were strangers near me but it didn't feel,
Like they were people that I didn't know,
Because they too were feeling that terrible blow.
That the world experienced on Christmas Day,
When our saviour Jesus Christ had taken you away.
Your house still stood in the same place,
Your fans were waiting to see your face.
We stared at the Windows hoping and praying,
That we had heard rumours, what people were saying?

We really couldn't accept that you had gone,
Why George, why does it feel so wrong?
God looked down on you that winters night,
He wrapped his arms around you holding tight.
He whispered for you to follow him, you didn't take
much persuading,
But one thing that we know our love, is that you were
AMAZING.

1983

I remember back in 1983,
I was bouncing my daughter around on my knee.
The radio was always playing behind,
It was always of *Wham*; they were one of a kind.
We listened to it all the time my baby and me,
She had learned the words to most of the songs by the
age of three.
Her sister she was born in 1984,
So, now there was the three of us to boogie on the floor.
Club Tropicana was a favourite to which we liked to
dance,
Careless whisper was the one that placed us all in a
trance.
As the years went by, George pursued a solo career,
Initially, that wasn't the news the *Wham* fans wanted to
hear.
But you know what, he excelled himself, his words
were from his heart,
Therefore, it was the best decision that they chose to
part.
His music became so heartfelt, we knew he meant every
single word,

Once you had listened to his songs, they were the best
that were ever heard.
You were amazing George, we just wished you really
knew,
Then your path in life may have dissuaded you from
life's choices that weren't true.
They say we learn the hard way, is that really what we
do?
Because you had everything George, so we really
haven't got a clue.

One Month On

It's been a month since that tragic day,
When someone or something stole you away.
Our hearts are sore they are ripped in two,
Why or why did it have to be you?
We just wish we could see your caring smile, and hear
your beautiful voice,
But we know we can't and that hurts so bad, we just
wish that we still had that choice.
George, did you not understand how much you were
loved by everyone?
My god we're all finding it hard accepting that you are
now gone.
If only on that Christmas night,
Before you laid in your bed and whispered good night.
You would have resisted the evil that was all around,
Instead you were tempted by what you found.
We will never know the truth behind that Christmas
Eve,
But what we want to know is, why did fadi leave?
We are searching for answers to help us all deal,
With the loss of you it's just so surreal.
All we have left are the memories of our wonderful icon
humble and kind,
We just wish you would have known the heartache that

you have left behind.

Sleep tight George while ever we breath, you will never be forgotten.

So Proud

When we close our eyes all that we can see is your
beautiful face, we know that this should make us happy
but instead it makes us sad,
Because we know it's just a memory of the lovely man
that we once had.
You were so kind, considerate and a very genuine guy,
You gave out generous gifts, some to people passing by.
Your family must have been so proud of all the love that
you had won,
But my god they will be broken at the loss of their
brother and son.
I believe that you were spiritual and I wanted to ask you
this,
If it's true, and you're in heaven send us a sign it doesn't
have to be a kiss.
Every hour of every day, in fact every second every
minute,
We miss you here on earth and wish you were back on
it.
Your kindness just shone through you, you were humble
and so kind,
Now we your fans are struggling as a greater man we

will never find.
We adored your wonderful music every lyric every
note,
It was the most amazing work and it never struggled to
be bought.
Your songs are selling really fast since you left us all,
In fact, most stores have sold out we constantly have to
call,
You will be number one again of that there is no doubt,
Especially when your new work will eventually come
out.

Rest in peace our beautiful Angel.

Your Worth

It's been a month now George since you left this earth,
If only you would have truly known your worth.
If you could only see the devastation that you left
behind,
Would you think that we were all out of our minds?
We're hurting so much George, it's really so hard,
Our hearts are broken and our minds are scarred.
We would give all we had George, to have you back
here,
Even if it was just for one more year.
Forgive us if you don't agree,
But we've so much to say to you, you see.
We want to tell you how much you meant,
Because to all your lovelies, you were the kindest gent.
We go to bed every night but just can't seem to rest,
As in our minds all we can think is that George you
were the best.
The world will never be the same,
Our hearts will sink when we hear your name.
We will look to the stars every night,
Then squeeze our pillows extra tight.
As the tears still continue to flow,

We all just want you to know.
We will never ever forget that day,
When you were so cruelly taken away.
Christmas Day 2016,
Will always be the worst day in history.
Goodbye seems so hard to say,
So, we will save that for another day.
When, we your fans, feel a little bit stronger,
As we needed you with us for a little while longer.

Free

Gorgeous George you are now set free,
Away from all of your misery.
No one will ever know what went through your mind,
It must have been so difficult to leave the drugs behind.
But what must have been more difficult for you,
Was to carry on as normal, because no one had a clue.
If only you would have been more open,
Expressing your sadness by being outspoken.
We would have wanted to help our beautiful boy,
The one whose music has brought us so much joy.
We cannot imagine life without you here,
Your music was our pleasure each and every year.
We know that if you realised the devastation you had
left,
It would never have happened we wouldn't be bereft.
Thank you for our memories, George, we will treasure
them so much,
You always delivered your music with a very special
touch.
Your voice was like an Angels, pitch perfect every time,
The words had so much meaning, every single line.
All we can do is hope and pray,
That happiness will come your way.

Up in heaven with the ones you love,
Goodbye George we send our love, to our beautiful soul
in heaven above.

The Crash

We remember that time when you crashed into the shop,
You walked out of your car and awaited the cops.
You are only human, George, just like the rest of us,
Why did they make it headlines and create a lot of fuss?
You admitted that for a while you hadn't mentally been
well,
Therefore, you used some substances what was the
major issue we wish that they would tell.
We know that it wasn't easy being as famous as you
were,
But in light of everything you appeared to handle this
without much of a care.
We admired you George and didn't really mind,
What you did in your private life we just wanted to stay
kind.
That's what loyal fans always tend to do,
Support you in many things that you had to go through.
You spoke about your demons but we never understood,
But then again I suppose with little information we
never would.
Please listen to us George, please try and understand,
We know you are in heaven but we need a helping hand.

Would it be possible for you to send a sign,
And let us know your happy just this one last time?
We didn't care about your past or whether you had a
husband or a wife,
We just need to know you're happy now then we can
carry on with our lives.

Infectious

George, when you were just a young man you drove all
the women wild,
Your looks, your style, your swagger, your amazing hair
and the way you smiled.
Your laugh was so infectious your personality shone
through,
Now all that has gone, what are we going to do?
You were someone so special whom we never will
forget,
Even though most of your fans you never even met.
But that just wasn't necessary as we had you on our
tellies,
Would we turn you off? no not on your Nellie.
Your voice was just pitch perfect, you always delivered
so well,
Fantastic George, you were so humble your head never
seemed to swell.
You covered up your heartache but we heard it in your
songs,
How sad that you somehow didn't know where you
belonged.
Your mum she was your best friend, her loss was very

hard,
But you managed to carry on with her picture on a card.
We fans are going to miss you, George, that is really
true,
We just cannot imagine what your family's going
through.
Take some rest now George, it's what you've really
earned,
We your fans are really sad that tables can't be turned.

Home

Well wouldn't it be good if we got in our car,
And travelled to George; our super pop star.
And when we arrived at his home by the river,
His door would open and we would all quiver.
Because there stood right in front of our eyes,
Would be our dear George handsome and wise.
He would walk to his gate and he would welcome us in,
We would have on our face the biggest of grins.
He would show us around his beautiful home,
With his chair in the lounge that he calls his throne.
He would make us a tea and be pleasant and kind,
And this would then confirm what's in all of our minds.
But sadly this just won't ever be,
As all we have left, is his memory.
We can pray, we can hope, we can try to accept,
But reality is he just isn't coming back.
George, George listen to us
Look down on earth and see all the fuss.
Look at the grief that is upon us all,
Has the world ever been this sad, I don't seem to recall.
How do we heal please send us a sign?
Maybe you can 'take us back in time',

God, the pain it hurts so much,
We just wanted to have one last touch.
If only this could be a bad dream,
And our eyes could dry instead of stream.
But Thank you George, for all that you gave,
We have your music we can all save.
A miracle lived with us here on earth,
You were meant to be special right from your birth.
We miss you George and we always will,
So, good night and God bless RIP until.
We one day will meet up in heaven above,
And you will just see the outpouring of love.
Sweet dreams our beautiful talented man,
You have some making up to do now with your lovely
mam.

Losing You

If only this could have been a careless whisper and that
it wasn't true,
Because hearts have been so broken George, over the
loss of you.
George, where are you now it's like Jesus to a child,
The carefree days are no more, the times when you were
wild.
You weren't just a talent you were so beautiful too,
One of our most admired legends you have gone far too
soon.
Take me back in time George, we won't forget,
Why didn't you turn a different corner? and something
different you may have met.
Whoever really cared George, if you were straight, gay
or bi,
The big question now is why, why, why?
Young Guns, *Club Tropicana* and many, many more,
Are classics that will stay with our children, their
children and many more.
Since you passed we got to hear about the kindness that
you gave,
To give the much less fortunate funds they could never

save.
Charities, students, couples probably others too,
But this was never publicised was this really hard to do.
Your much-loved passion was to rid the world of AIDS,
You must have been so proud of all the lives that you
have saved.
Musician, artist, composer, song writer, singer,
gentleman, compassionate, considerate and kind,
These are the beautiful memories you have kindly left
behind.
Rest in peace George, you are finally free,
Your talent will live on in us each and every day,
The sun finally came down on you George, it's your
time to wander free,
All we have left of you now is your legacy.
So, ladies and gentleman let's pay our respects,
To the most adored person who never got to see his *Last
Christmas*.

Respects

I've come down to Goring to pay my respects,
To an all-time legend who I never met.
It's a beautiful town this place that I'm in,
But my heart is ripped in two, a wish it wasn't him.
I can see why he liked to live down here,
It's right posh and it's got nice beer.
His house is a beauty right on the river,
There are flowers and tributes that are making me
quiver.
There is only one comfort I can get from all this, is that
he just went to sleep,
He knew nothing about it but it's sad we couldn't keep.
The music legend who gave so much pleasure,
To his loyal fans now they can treasure.
The much-loved memories he has left behind,
Cos by the good night he was one of a kind.

Unresolved

There was once a man who lived here on earth,
We don't think he ever understood his worth.
His name it was George, he was beautiful and kind,
No other man like him in this world will we find.
He wrote beautiful music that came from his heart,
He had a beautiful spirit that we didn't want to depart.
But one wicked, horrid Christmas Day,
We heard the tragic news that he'd been taken away.
He was all alone in his beautiful house,
It must have been so silent not even a mouse.
When something happened but we will never know,
This causes us heartache and makes our tears flow.
George we have so many questions we fans want to ask,
What happened that night, what was your last task?
Did you have a fight with the love of your life?
Did he end it all and that made you decide,
That enough was enough, and you really couldn't take,
Just one more day for anyone's sake?
If this was your choice then we must all respect,
That your wish came true you were really hen pecked.
But if it was an accident then we also respect that too,
Because you chose to take drugs, so we accept that was

you,
However, George you know we're broken,
Many good words have been recently spoken.
You were our legend, our idol our friend,
We never knew you personally but we loved you till the
end.
We hope you're up in heaven safe in your mother's
arms,
That you are telling her all she missed from the day she
did depart.
As I write this poem just for you, the tears roll down my
cheeks,
When I think about the memories you left my body feels
so weak.
God George, if only you could come back to all who
love you so,
Because if you could, one things for sure, we would
never let you go.
It's unbearable to think of all your families' pain,
Because we didn't have you in our lives, but we loved
you just the same.
Why has God decided that it was your time to go?
If he would just have asked around he knows too well
the answer would be no.
He usually takes the best ones first that's always been
the case,
But we just wished he could have left you longer so we
could see your beautiful face.

RIP George Michael
1963-2016
Goodbye legend

Wham

I think it was 1981 when *Wham* came on the scene,
Girls hearts were a flutter, were these two guys a dream.
I was the same age as the two boys from *Wham*,
I used to sing their music all the time according to me
mam.
I had a daughter when they were around,
Then I had another so I was house bound.
I would play their records all night and day,
My girls they loved them too, that's what they used to
say.
The lyrics of their songs they always seemed just right,
They became addictive every morning, noon and night.
They got on well together all the group named *Wham*,
Until George decided to go solo, that was quite a bang.
But you know what? He did it and he amazed us all,
His vocals and his music made us all stand tall.
Thank you for your music George, it will never ever die,
Unlike you, you've left us all we just wished it was a lie.

Love Again

(Rewording to Careless Whisper)

Time will never mend the news,
We heard of the death of our legend, it broke our hearts
in two.
What are we going to do?
It's so hard to carry on without you.
We're never going to laugh again,
Broken hearts are just not amending.
Even when we try to pretend,
It's still so hard to do,
we're never going to laugh again. Broken hearts are just
not mending, no we never going to laugh again. The
way we laughed with you.
George why didn't you say,
You were hurt so much it didn't go away.
It came as such a shock, it was all so new,
Christmas days of all the days why did it have to be
you?
We're never going to love again,
Broken hearts are just not mending,
We're never going to love again the way we loved with

you,
No we're never going to love again we all know we're
just pretending,
No we're never going to love again the way we loved
with you.
You were one of a kind,
A humble man with a troubled mind,
Why couldn't anyone help,
Was it really too late?
We as fans aren't bearing up, the pain is just too great.
We're never going to live the same,
Broken hearts are just not mending,
Our lives will never be the same.
We just don't know what to do,
we're never going to live again the way we lived with
you.

The News

We remember it well it was Christmas Day night, we
came and we laid in our bed,
We looked at our phones and could not believe, it was
saying that George you were dead.
Can you ever imagine that pain when your heart is just
ripped in two?
How can life ever be the same without the love of you?
We messaged my friends we wanted their views,
We just wanted confirmation of this horrific news.
It almost felt like we had been stunned, we really
couldn't comprehend,
Our love, our life, our hero, our beautiful best friend,
Where was he now, was he really gone, was this really
the end?
Pain, sorrow, heart ache, hurt, tears,
What an impact you have left on us over the years.
Every single emotion was going through our mind,
It surely wasn't true; you were one of a kind.
The last time I experienced pain so bad,
Was when I lost my brother and my mum and dad.
Everything was flooding back it was so hard to believe,
Why, why, why did you have to leave?

Your fans are truly sad,
It feels surreal we are going mad.
We didn't want this to be true,
All we wanted was to still be here with you.

From Heaven

When we look to the sky above and look into the
clouds,
We try to imagine you are there staring at the crowds.
We wonder if you ever really knew,
How much love that the whole world had for you.
The rich, the poor, the in between,
Even the famous including our queen.
Have all been touched by your untimely death,
It came far too early you should never have left.
We never will get over this whilst we are here on earth,
You've touched so many lives and made us realise your
worth.
We really won't get over this it's ever so surreal,
We wonder if our hearts will ever fully heal.
They say that grief takes time and none of us grieve the
same,
But George our hearts are breaking every time we hear
your name.
Our love for you is loyal and kind,
Just like the memories that you left behind.
Every song you made was a treasure,
Each one gave us so much pleasure.

Thank you for that George as that is what we have left,
From our beautiful legend that left us bereft.

Gentle Soul

Gentle and soul are two of the words that we can relate
to you,
Your music always reflected just what you needed to
do.
You couldn't express the amount of love you held deep
within your heart,
But your music helped you deliver this right from the
start.
There have been many performers in the music industry,
But clearly not as special as you would always be.
Your presence out on the stage was always mass
perfection,
The emotion that you displayed always won our
affection.
Our gentle soul how passionate you would be,
Our hair would stand on end and we would set ourselves
free.
Your voice was always very clear and really precise,
There was nothing or no one in the world that's ever
been that nice.
Our gentle soul has left us but were mostly in denial,
We're waiting for the outcome of your death it's like a
trial.

We hope that there is nothing found, no evidence to
suggest,
That foul play would have happened, or it will end up to
be a mess.
Our gentle beautiful soul, you are impossible to replace,
God we fans are missing you and your beautiful face.
Why did you leave, why did you go?
We really don't think that we will ever really know.
If love could bring you back on earth, you would be
here today,
We would keep you close to all of us and never let you
stray.
We need you George back here with us,
We promise we won't make a fuss.

Please come home.

Remembering You

Guess what George, I'm sure you would like to know,
That we your lovelies continue to grow.
There is a social media site all in the memory of you,
And it has helped us all through our grief of losing you.
Every day, every hour in fact quite possibly every
minute,
There is something new posted and it's got you in it.
We your lovelies just can't accept that you are here no
more,
We've cried so much about you our hearts are so, so
sore.
There is people from all over the world that grieve for
you right now,
If only you could see this, we don't think you would
believe it somehow.
You know George we can listen to your music, we can
also hear your voice,
And if loving could have saved you, that would have
been our choice.
Australia, New Zealand, Canada, America, the list goes
on and on,
The people in these countries want to know just what
went wrong.

It appeared you had ordered shopping and was to
prepare a festive lunch,
So, what happened next seems like an almighty punch.
Because the blow that we your fans received,
Has left us so very deeply intrigued.
Something has happened something's not right,
Did you and your lover end up in a fight?
We guess whatever happened we would never get to
know,
But we your lovelies on this site will continue to grow
and grow.

Letting You Know

We your loving fans that are left to feel the pain,
Need to let you know that things will never be the same.
Our hearts are so broken they are actually ripped in two,
Nothing will ever be as bad as the pain of losing you.
Then we think if we feel this sad,
What about your family, your sisters and your dad?
Their pain must be unbearable, how can they ever deal,
With knowing that the tragic news they heard that day
was real?
We can only try to empathise with what they are going
through,
Because they lost a huge piece of their lives the day that
they lost you.
We your lovelies want them to know that they are not
alone,
As we share their pain every day since our Lord God
took you home.
So gentle Jesus up above,
Send our George all our love.
We hope that you will let him rest,
Because he quite simply was the best.
Tell him that we loved him, tell him that we cared,
And thank him for his memories that we his fans have
shared.

It's Hard

It's hard, everything is hard, it's hard watching you sing,
It's hard watching you dance or do anything.
Our mind feels like we are going crazy,
When we think of your death, our brain becomes hazy.
We think that's because you are still around,
We can watch you on YouTube and still hear your
sounds.
It's so damn hard George everything we see,
Are constant reminders of what it should be.
We wanted you with us here on earth,
To see you as an old man and for you to appreciate your
worth.
But as the days pass we now know you won't be back,
And this becomes so hard to keep our emotions on
track.
God George, it really is so hard, will we ever be able to
smile,
Because we can assure you it's been a while.
We really need to tell you that we miss you so, so bad,
You were the best entertainer this world has ever had.
So, if you're up there looking down and can see the hurt
and pain,

Please understand all our feelings and emotions are not in vain.
We just want you back with us and we're sure your family would agree,
But instead you've taken your angel wings and decided to wander free.

Rest in eternal peace our angel

Grammys

Well we waited with anticipation not knowing what we
would see,
Then Adele came on singing your song in quite a low
key.
She struggled with the music she just didn't get it right,
But she didn't want to ruin it she knew it was your night.
She had another attempt and we must say that it was
better,
She wanted to do careless whisper but the producers
wouldn't let her.
We all had different opinions, some loved it yet some
didn't,
But We have to say Adele you were definitely a winner,
How hard it must have been to stand there live on stage,
And perform your good friend's song you were all the
rage.
Thank you Adele you did him proud I'm sure that he
was there,
Your emotion was so evident you displayed how much
you cared.
I bet his families were distraught when they watched the
show,

I perceived that you too didn't want to let him go.
We all have wonderful memories of our idol, our legend
our friend,
But for you, all in the industry will your hearts ever
mend.
The video in the background made us really sad and cry,
Because we can't have George back and we will always
wonder why.
That he had to leave his loved ones to spend our time on
earth,
Whilst he is up in heaven not knowing what he was
worth.
But once again, thank you Adele it couldn't have been
so easy,
You're such a lovely lady, beautiful not sleazy.
But one other thing that his lovelies really wanted to
see,
Was George Michael collecting a Grammy to put with
his other three.

Beautiful Guy

George, George, George our beautiful guy,
Who was humble and patient and never did lie.
Why didn't the media ever leave you alone?
They were like mongrels after the bone.
They were quick to report all of your wrong,
But never seemed to praise your wonderful songs.
Look at what you went through out in the states,
They almost lost you, all your mates.
Everyone is allowed their freedom of speech,
But they went in for you just like a leech,
If you wanted to write straight from your heart,
What was their problem, why did it all start?
They never reported all the good that you have done,
But immediately homed in on your times of having fun.
But you know what, we as devoted fans,
Didn't care less about all their plans.
We never saw anything bad in you George,
The reason for that was there was none of course.
Humble, gentle, patient, generous and kind,
These are a few of the memories you left behind.
Rest in peace now George in heaven above,
Take with you our hearts that are full of love.

We cherish every memory here on earth,
And believe me, we your loyal fans understood your worth.

As Time Goes By

We thought it would get easier as the days turned into
weeks,
But honestly it's just not true as the tears fall on our
Cheeks.
We think about you all the time, we wonder where
you've gone,
We think of all the memories they help us carry on.
George, we want to let you know how hard it is down
here,
We know that we will still feel the pain as the months
turn into years.
Sometimes it seems impossible as to why it hurts so
bad,
We wonder why the pain still lingers and why we still
feel sad.
We cry when we are all alone it seems to help us cope,
Some people think we're crazy they really are a joke.
What can be so hard for them to not understand our
pain,
It really isn't fair; we want you here to love again.
If you could only understand why we hurt so much,
It's because we know we're never going to ever feel
your touch.

We miss you George every single day,
We don't think the hurt will ever go away.
So, until we all will meet again,
We will continue to try and manage our pain.

When You Left

We want to know George, if on that Christmas Eve,
You went to bed knowing that this earth you were about
to leave.
We wonder if when you closed your eyes you just
wanted to fall to sleep,
Or did you plan to leave this life knowing you weren't
ours to keep.
We will never really know what happened on that
Christmas night,
The only one that can tell us isn't here it's just not right.
Something doesn't fit well with us your heart broken
fans,
If we remember rightly you had made some future
plans.
Why is the outcome taking so long? The suspense is
killing us all,
We want to hear the answers of that night when you
were called.
We picture you on an island with loved ones by your
side,
The tears that have fallen down our face are not really
what we've cried.
But we can't go on pretending that you are still here

with all your fans,
Because reality is finally hitting us all and no one will
ever replace our man,
As we close our eyes and imagine you up above,
We see white clouds and angels smothering you with
love,
But just because you are up there and not here with us
on earth.,
No longer affects how much we love and appreciate
your worth.

Tragedy

We all have had tragedy in our lives, some much worse
than others,
But Christmas Day was one of the hardest, it was as
painful as losing our mothers.
We sit at home trying to remain the same,
When all of a sudden someone mentions your name.
Our hearts skip a beat and our eyes fill with tears,
We accept now, that this pain will be with us for years.
Last Christmas I gave you my heart,
These words will be with us till death do us part.
How ironic of all the days in the year,
You left us so tragically it's frightening we fear.
That someday in the very near future something will be
said,
Perhaps it's not the news we would like as really we
wouldn't want you dead.
But some of us have come to accept that the cause of
your death was ill health,
Some of us think that your lifestyle contributed and that
was part of your wealth.
Some of us think that there is something more to it and
those of us want to find out,

Because we just can't accept that you left us that day, of that there is no doubt.
We know you didn't like the press and all the trouble they gave,
But George, if it wasn't for them, we wouldn't have pictures to save.
Please George forgive us if we feel torn,
If our hearts are broken and our shoes are worn.
With pacing the floor as anxiety strikes,
It's not very nice it's not something we like.
But it's almost like panic takes over our days,
Most of the hours are spent in a haze.
Our thoughts are transfixed on you and only you,
We toss and turn and lie awake just wishing it weren't true.
We have many years ahead of us to carry all this pain,
My god, dear George, we thank the lord, we will never go through this again.

Feel the Pain

For how much longer do we feel the pain?
The tears continue to flow like heavy rain.
Our eyes are sore from wiping them dry,
Why George did you have to die?
How could you have been so sad?
The whole world loved you, you were never bad.
It didn't matter to us what you did,
All that mattered was that you continued to live.
We didn't care if you were fat or thin or even in
between,
We just wanted you to entertain us, sing and dance and
make a scene.
Come on George, let us know that you didn't die in vain,
Let us know that if you could, you would entertain us all
again.
We thought that as the months passed by the pain would
disappear,
But that's never going to happen because you're no
longer here.
We only have our memories that will stay with us until
we die,
Unfortunately, George, we are sad to say we your fans

continue to cry.
We have tried to heal our pain but it just doesn't seem to
go,
So, for now we will continue to feel upset and very low.

Perception of The World

My perception of the world is that it was such a happy
place,
But I don't have the same perception since we don't
have your beautiful face.
Everyone has experienced a loss beyond all measure,
But we have special memories of you George that we
can treasure.
It's been many months now that you were taken away,
We will never ever forget the news that we got to hear
that day.
There's just one thing that could possibly be true,
And that is that this earth wasn't meant for beautiful
you.
You were too perfect in every single way,
That's why we believe that on earth you couldn't stay.
Forgive the fact that we still grieve for you our precious
man,
However, we will continue to support each other the
very best that we can.